Walter Crane, Edmund Evans

Bluebeard's Picture Book

Containing: Bluebeard, The Sleeping Beauty And Baby's Own Alphabet

Walter Crane, Edmund Evans

Bluebeard's Picture Book
Containing: Bluebeard, The Sleeping Beauty And Baby's Own Alphabet

ISBN/EAN: 9783744651622

Printed in Europe, USA, Canada, Australia, Japan

Cover: Foto ©Thomas Meinert / pixelio.de

More available books at **www.hansebooks.com**

BLUEBEARD'S · PICTURE BOOK ·

CONTAINING
BLUEBEARD
THE SLEEPING BEAU
TY,   AND
BABY'S OWN ALPHA
BET
WITH THE ORIGINAL
COLOURED DESIGNS
BY
WALTER CRANE.
ENGRAVED & PRINTED BY
EDMUND EVANS

LONDON & NEW YORK: JOHN LANE THE BODLEY HEAD

·PREFACE·

LUEBEARD'S key, no doubt, unlocked many mysteries, and he may have had among his treasures a picture-book, if only to amuse his wives with, or to divert their attention from his own dark designs: but it must not be supposed that BLUEBEARD. although he is not free from the suspicion of having put several beauties to sleep - in presenting himself again with THE SLEEPING BEAUTY is at all responsible for her enchanted slumber, or that either BLUEBEARD or THE SLEEPING BEAUTY are concerned with BABY'S OWN ALPHABET- except for the spelling of their own names.

These time honoured personages must, in their present form be rather regarded as the figures in the antique tapestry which decorates the storied walls of the festive nursery guest hall, where His Baby ship invites, by his letters patent, a motley company of old friends in fancy dress for his disport, and for the pleasure of all contemporary despots of the rattle, not to speak of the larger baby-public content to look over the heads on the front bench.

Or, 'an it may please you, we may take, as the more natural order our A.B.C. first (as indeed we should) to represent the "curtain raiser" - something light and playful before the heavy tragedy of BLUEBEARD, & the fairy romance of THE SLEEPING BEAUTY   It is all one - at least they are all in one book now: and it is hoped, both by artist and publisher, that they will "fill the bill", and draw the baby-public, small and great, as of old.

At all events one may feel certain that when BABY has learnt his OWN ALPHABET he will be sure to demand a book of the words - so here it is.

Streatley-on-Thames. Aug: 1899.

WALTER·CRANE'S·PICTURE·BOOKS·REISSUE·

BLUE BEARD

LONDON·&·NEW·YORK·JOHN·LANE·THE·BODLEY·H?

BLUEBEARD.

ONCE on a time there lived a man
  hated by all he knew,
Both that his ways were very bad,
  and that his beard was blue;
But as he was so rich and grand, and
  led a merry life,
A lady he contrived at last to induce
  to be his wife.

For a month after the wedding they
    lived and had good cheer;
And then said Bluebeard to his wife,
    "I'll say good bye, my dear.
"Indeed, it is but for six weeks that I
    shall be away,
"I beg that you'll invite your friends,
    and feast and dance and play;
"And all my property I'll leave con-
    fided to your care;
"Here are the keys of all my chests,
    there's plenty and to spare."

" But this small key belongs to one small
    room on the ground-floor,—
" And this you must not open, or you
    will repent it sore."
And so he went; and all the friends
    came there from far and wide,
And in her wealth the lady took much
    happiness and pride;
But in a while this kind of joy grew
    nearly satisfied,

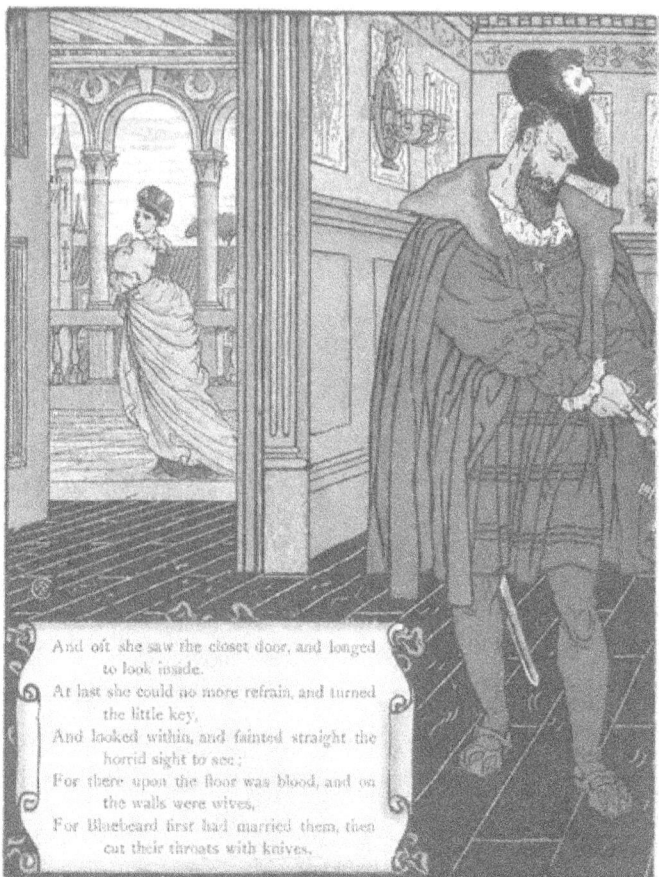

And oft she saw the closet door, and longed
to look inside.
At last she could no more refrain, and turned
the little key,
And looked within, and fainted straight the
horrid sight to see;
For there upon the floor was blood, and on
the walls were wives,
For Bluebeard first had married them, then
cut their throats with knives.

And this poor wife, distracted, picked the key
    up from the floor,
All stained with blood, and with much fear
    she shut and locked the door.
She tried in vain to clean the key and wash
    the stain away
With sand and soap,—it was no use. Blue
    beard came back that day.
At once he asked her for the key,—he saw
    the bloody stain,—

> "You have been in the closet once,
>   and you shall go again!"
> "O spare me, spare me! give me
>   time, nor kill me hastily!"
> "You have a quarter of an hour,—
>   then, madam, you must die!"
> "O sister Anne, go up, go up, and
>   look out from the tower;
> I'm dead unless my brothers come
>   in a quarter of an hour!"
> And Anne looked once, and Anne
>   looked twice, and nothing saw
>   abroad,
> But shining sun and growing grass,
>   and dust upon the road.

"Come down!" cried Bluebeard, "time is
     up!" With many a sigh and moan,
She prayed him for a minute more; he
     shouted still, "Come down!"
"O sister Anne, look out, look out! and do
     you nothing see?"
"At last I see our brothers two come riding
     hastily."
"Now spare me, Bluebeard,—spare thy
     wife!" but as the words were said,

And just as Bluebeard's cruel blade was
  descending on her head,
In rushed the brothers with their swords,—
  they cut the murderer down,
And saved their sister's life, and gained
  much glory and renown;
And then they all with gold and plate and
  jewels rare made free,
And ever after lived content on Bluebeard's property.

WALTER CRANE'S · PICTURE · BOOKS · RE·ISSUE ·

THE · SLEEPING · BEAUTY

LONDON · & · NEW·YORK · JOHN·LANE · THE · BODLEY · HEAD ·

·WALTER CRANE'S PICTURE·BOOKS—RE·ISSUE·
ENGRAVED & PRINTED IN COLOURS
BY EDMUND EVANS

BLUEBEA
PICTURE
BOOK

THE FOLLOWING MAY NOW BE HAD
IN THIS SERIES:
[SINGLE COPIES 1/- EACH, OR
BOUND IN SETS OF THREE 4/6 A VOL.]

THIS LITTLE PIG.
THE FAIRY SHIP.
KING LUCKIE BOY.

OLD MOTHER HUBBARD
THE THREE BEARS
THE ABSURD A.B.C.

CINDERELLA
PUSS IN BOOTS
VALENTINE & ORSON

LITTLE RED RIDING HOOD
JACK & THE BEAN STALK
THE FORTY THIEVES

BLUE BEARD
THE SLEEPING BEAUTY
THE BABY'S OWN
ALPHABET.

·LONDON·&·NEW·YORK·JOHN LANE·THE BODLEY HEAD·

THE SLEEPING BEAUTY.

L ONG, long ago, in ancient times, there lived a King and Queen,
And for the blessing of a child their longing sore had been;
At last, a little daughter fair, to their great joy, was given,
And to the christening feast they made, they bade the Fairies seven—

The Fairies seven, who loved the land—that they the child might bless,
Yet one old Fairy they left out, in pure forgetfulness.
And at the feast, the dishes fair were of the reddest gold;
But when the Fairy came, not one for her, so bad and old:
Angry was she, because her place and dish had been forgot,
And angry things she muttered long, and kept her anger hot.

Until the Fairy godmothers their gifts and wishes gave;
She waited long to spoil the gifts, and her revenge to have.
One gave the Princess goodness, and one gave her beauty rare;
One gave her sweetest singing voice; one, gracious mien and air;
One, skill in dancing; one, all cleverness; and then the crone
Came forth, and muttered, angry still, and good gift gave she none;

An aged peasant told of an enchanted palace, where
A sleeping King and Court lay hid, and sleeping Princess fair.
Through the thick wood, that gave him way, and past the thorns that drew
Their sharpest points another way, the King's son presses through.
He reached the guard, the court, the hall,—and there, where'er he stept,
He saw the sentinels, and grooms, and courtiers as they slept.

Ladies in act to smile, and pages in attendance wait;
The horses slept within their stalls, the dogs about the gate.
The King's son presses on, into an inner chamber fair,
And sees, laid on a silken bed, a lovely lady there;
So sweet a face, so fair—was never beauty such as this;
He stands—he stoops to gaze—he kneels—he wakes her with a kiss.

He leads her forth ; the magic sleep of all the Court is o'er,—
They wake, they move, they talk, they laugh, just as they did of yore,
A hundred years ago. The King and Queen awake, and tell
How all has happed, rejoicing much that all has ended well.
They hold the wedding that same day, with mirth and feasting good—
The wedding of the Prince and Sleeping Beauty in the Wood.

8

·WALTER·CRANE'S·PICTURE·BOOKS·RE·ISSUE·4¢²

·THE·BABY'S·OWN·
·ALPHABET·

LONDON & NEW·YORK· JOHN·LANE·THE·BODLEY·HEAD·

· WALTER CRANE'S · PICTURE · BOOKS - RE · ISSUE ·
ENGRAVED & PRINTED IN COLOURS
BY EDMUND EVANS

BLUEBEARD
PICTURE
BOOK

THE FOLLOWING MAY NOW BE HAD
IN THIS SERIES:
[SINGLE COPIES 1/- EACH, OR
BOUND IN SETS OF THREE 4/6 A VOL.]

THIS LITTLE PIG.
THE FAIRY SHIP.
KING LUCKIE BOY.

OLD MOTHER HUBBARD
THE THREE BEARS
THE ABSURD A.B.C.

CINDERELLA
PUSS IN BOOTS
VALENTINE & ORSON

LITTLE RED RIDING HOOD
JACK & THE BEAN STALK
THE FORTY THIEVES

BLUE BEARD
THE SLEEPING BEAUTY
THE BABY'S OWN
ALPHABET.

· LONDON & NEW YORK · JOHN LANE · THE BODLEY HEAD ·

A a
B b
C c
D d

AS I was going up Pippin Hill, Pippin Hill was dirty; There I met a pretty miss, And she dropped me a curtsy.

BOYS and girls come out to play, The moon doth shine as bright as day! Come with a whoop, come with a call, Come with a good will, or not at all.

Little Tommy Tittlemouse

CUCKOO, cherry tree Come down & tell me How many years I have to live

DING dong bell, Pussy's in the well Who put her in? Naughty Johnny Green Who pulled her out?

E e

F f

G g

EARLY to bed, and early to rise, | Is the way to be healthy, wealthy, and wise.

FOR every evil under the sun | If there be one, try and find it; There is a remedy, or there is none. | If there be none, never mind it.

GREAT A, little A, Bouncing B; The cat's in the cupboard, And she can't see me.

HARK! hark! the dogs do bark,
The beggars are coming to town,
Some in rags, some in jags,
And some in velvet gowns.

I HAD a little pony,
They called it Dapple Grey;
I lent it to a lady,
To ride a mile away;
She whipped it, she slashed it,
She drove it through the mire;
I will not lend my pony now
For all the lady's hire.

JOHN SMITH, fellow fine,
Can you shoe this horse o' mine?
Yes, indeed, and that I can,
As well as any man!
There's a nail upon the toe, &c.
To make the pony spank the snow;
There's a nail, and there's a prod,
And now, good-dame, your horse is shod.

3

K k

L l

M m

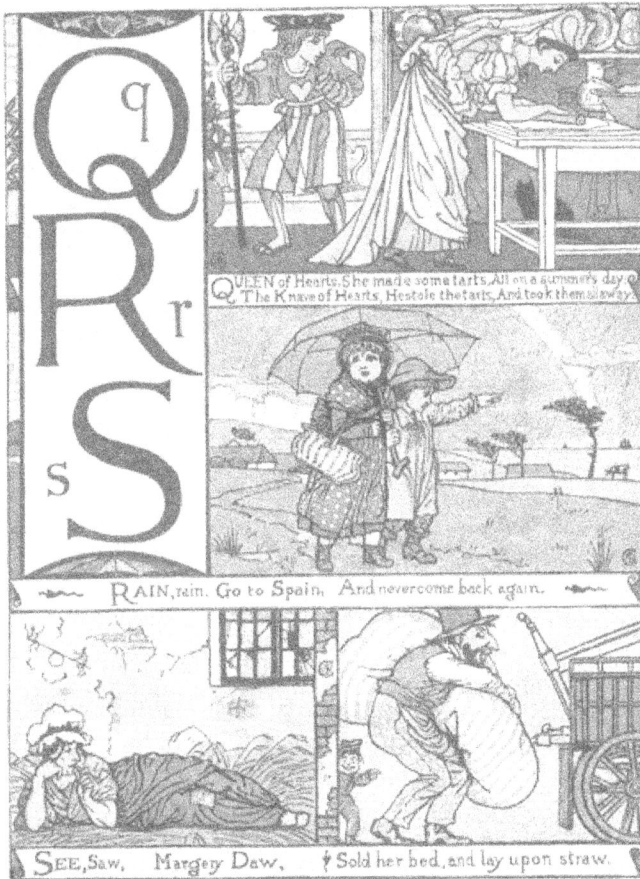

QUEEN of Hearts. She made some tarts, All on a summer's day.
The Knave of Hearts, He stole the tarts, And took them all away.

RAIN, rain. Go to Spain, And never come back again.

SEE, Saw, Margery Daw, Sold her bed, and lay upon straw.

T t
U u
V v

Three children sliding on the ice, As it fell out, they all fell in;
Upon a summer's day; The rest they ran away;

U Phill spare me, Downhill ware me, On level ground spare me not, And in the stable forget me not.

VALENTINE ✿ The rose is red; the Violet blue ✿ The pink is sweet; & so are you

7

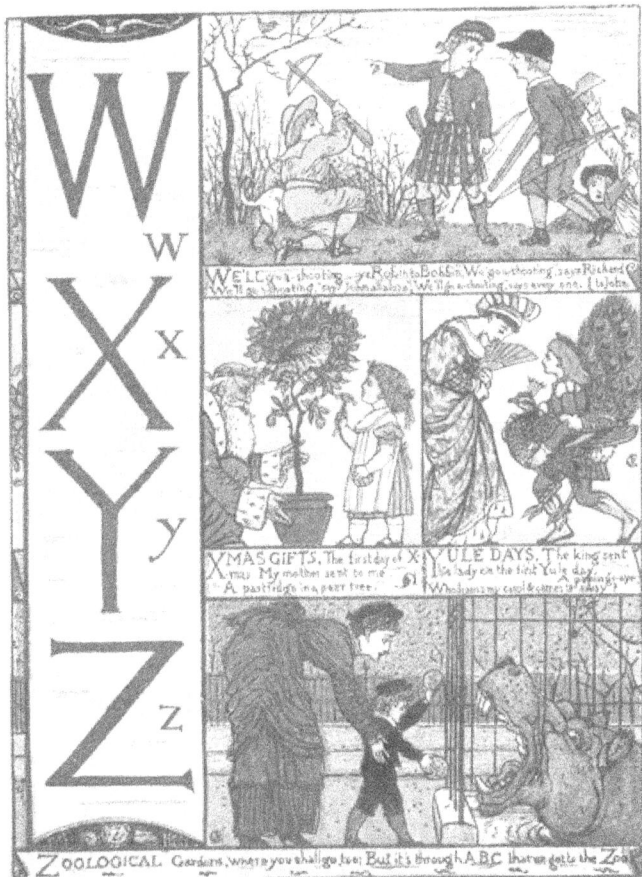

WE'LL go a shooting, says Robin to Bobbin. We go a shooting, says Richard to
We'll go a shooting, says John all alone. We'll go a shooting, says every one. {to John.

X MAS GIFTS. The first day of X
mas My mother sent to me
A partridge in a pear tree.

Y ULE DAYS. The king sent
his lady on the first Yule day,
Who sent my carol & carry it away?

Z OOLOGICAL Gardens, where you shall go too; But it's through A,B,C that we gets to the Zoo.

www.ingramcontent.com/pod-product-compliance
Lightning Source LLC
Chambersburg PA
CBHW021631270326
41931CB00008B/966